I0468751

Swear Word Coloring Book

SwearyStressRelief

SwearWord Adult Coloring Book

Ho Bag

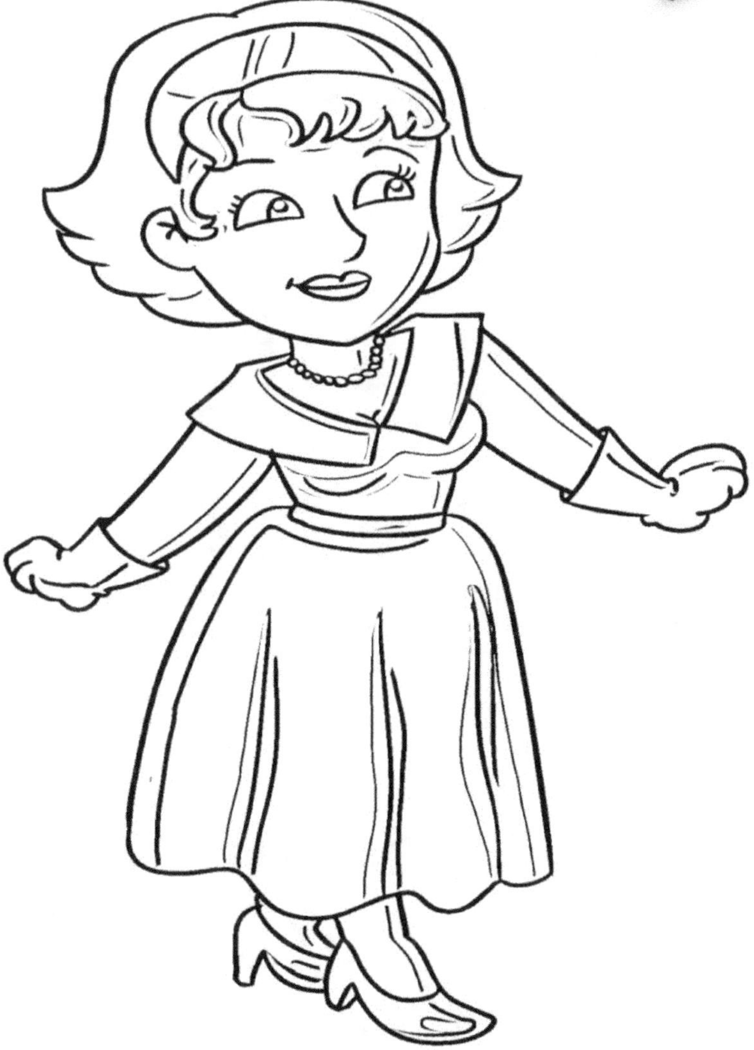

SquirtFace

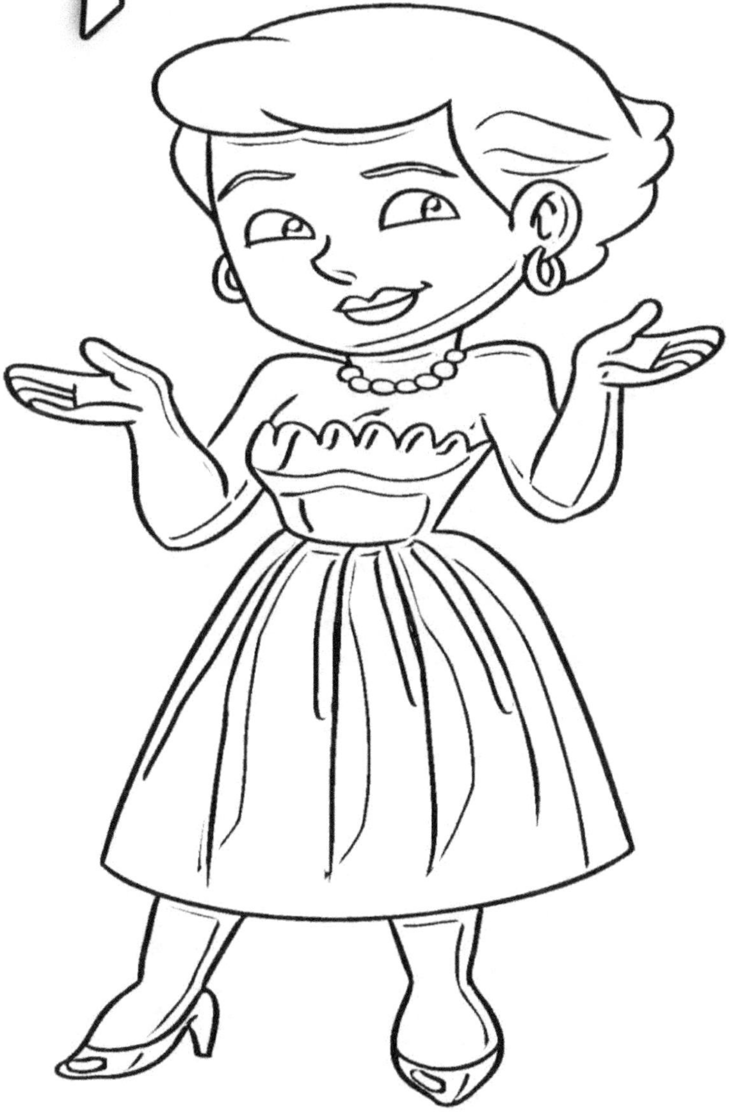

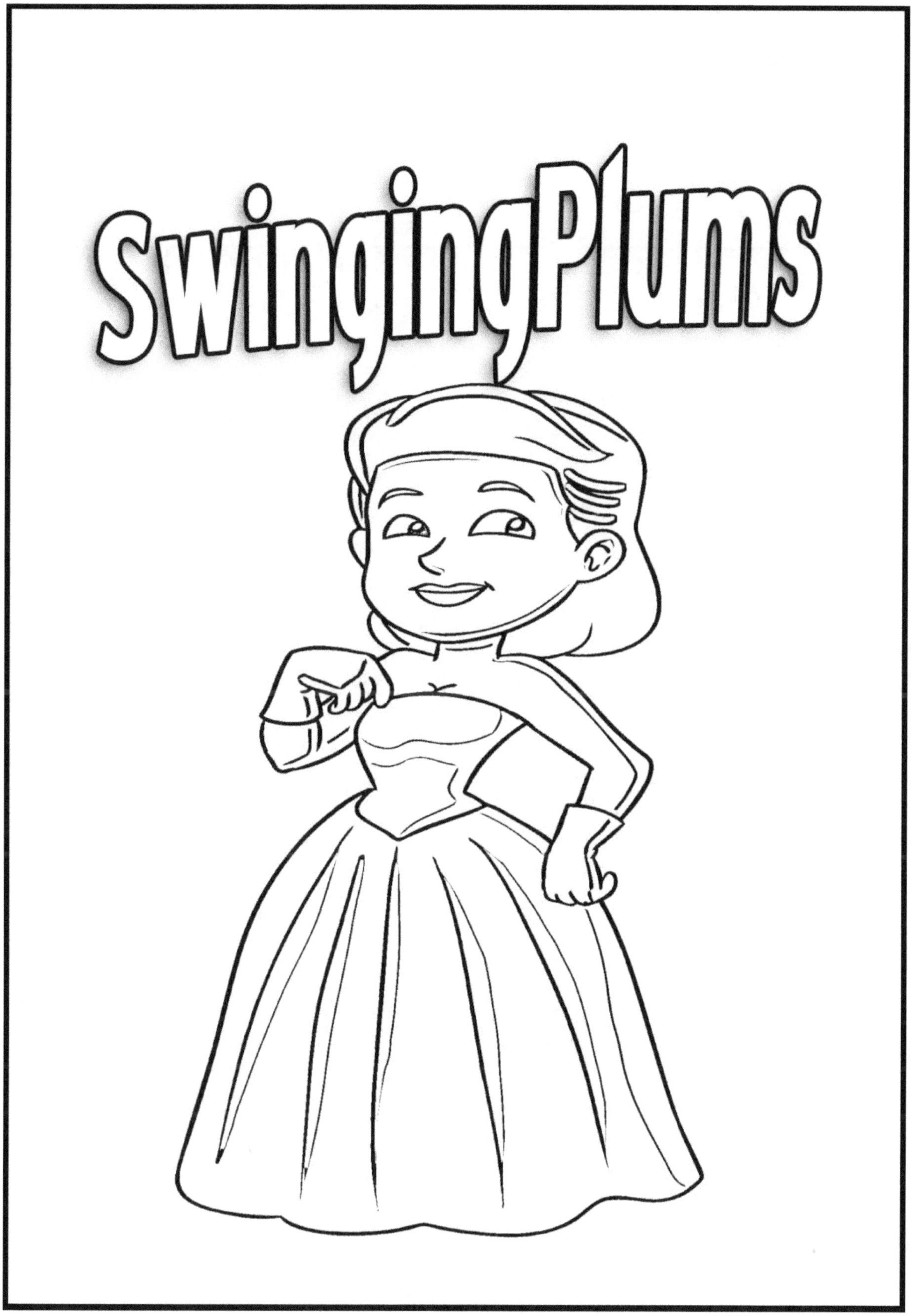
SwingingPlums

Ass Pirate

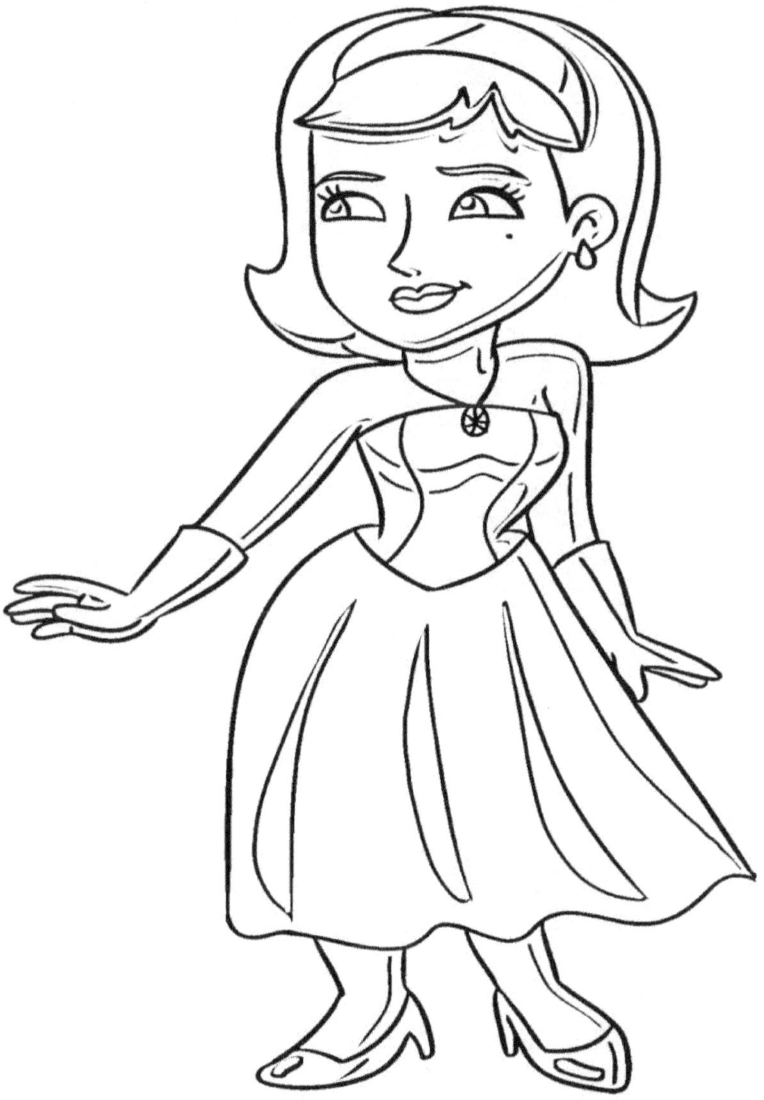

JizzDumpster

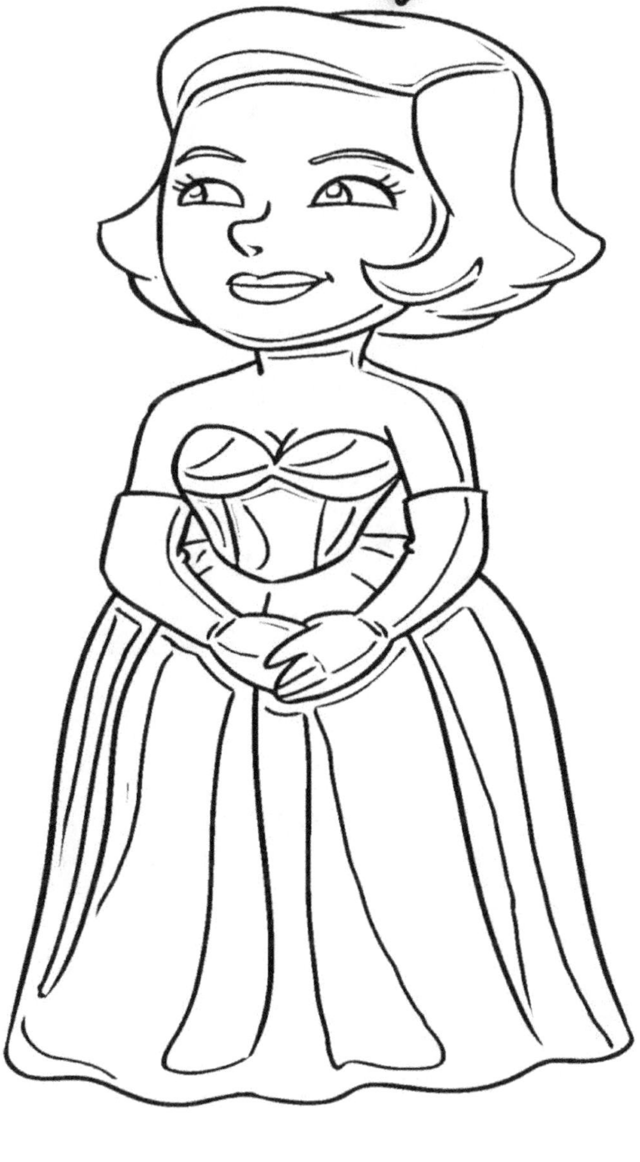

CumStain

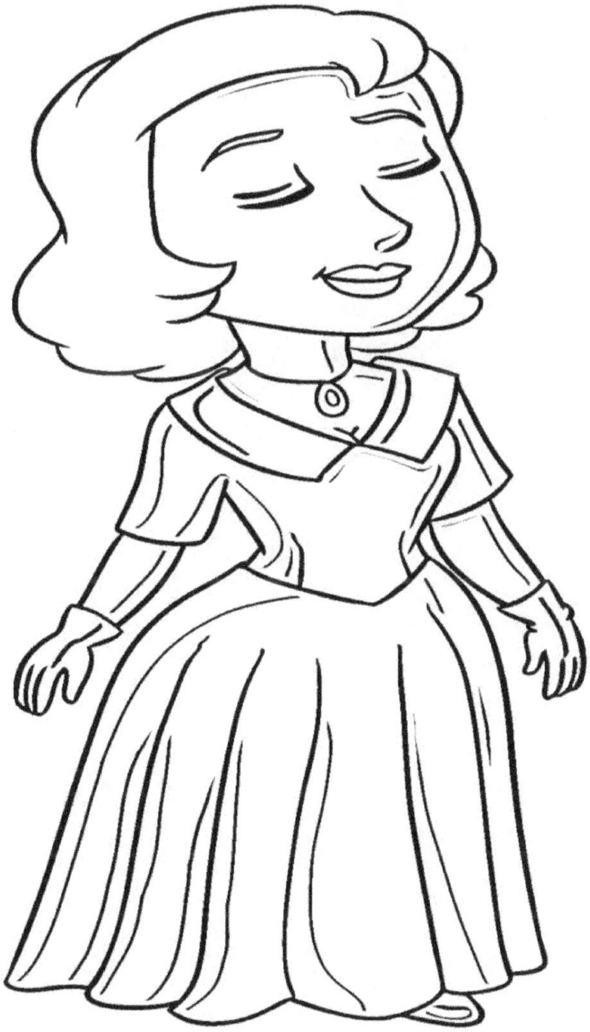

AssClap

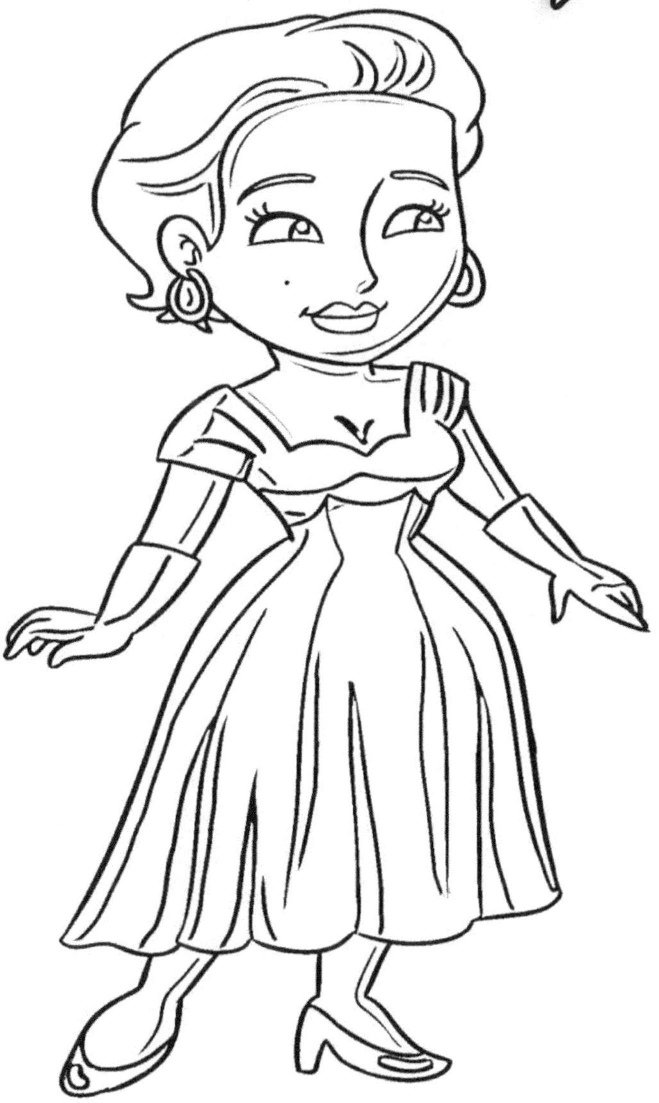

FuckHead

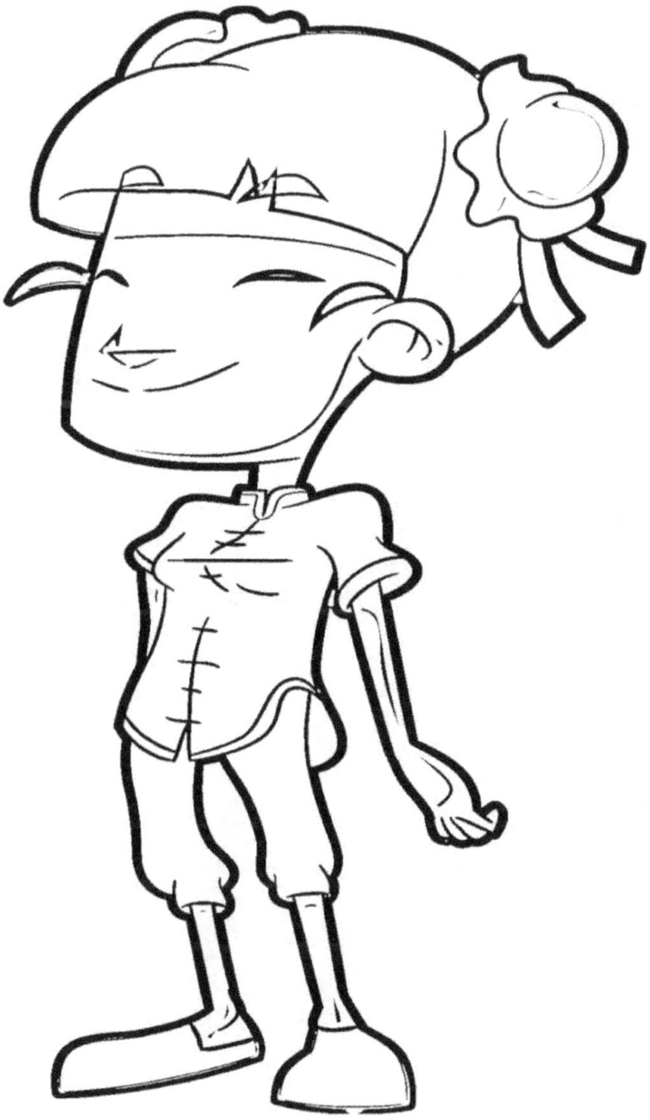

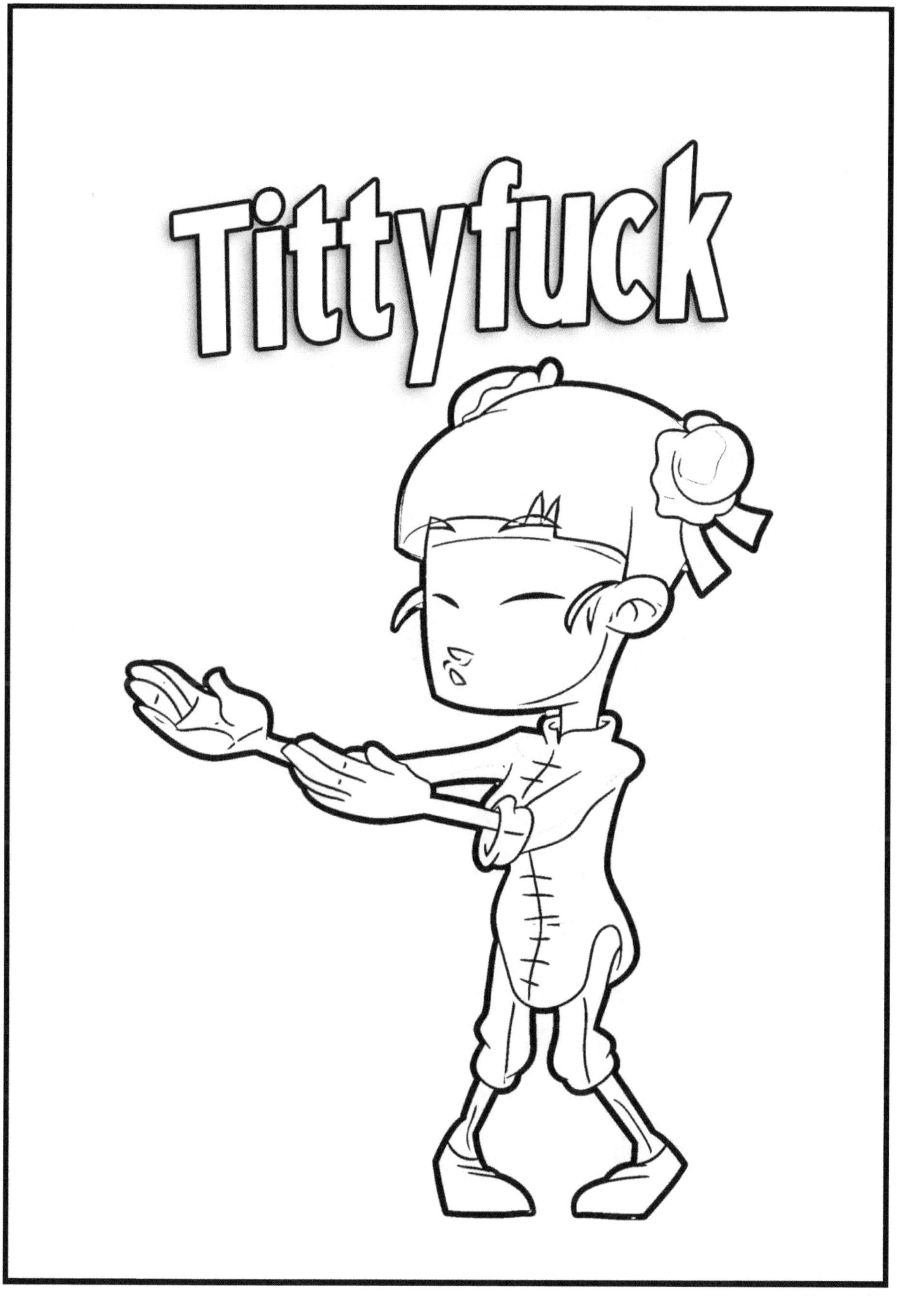
Tittyfuck

MeatBeater

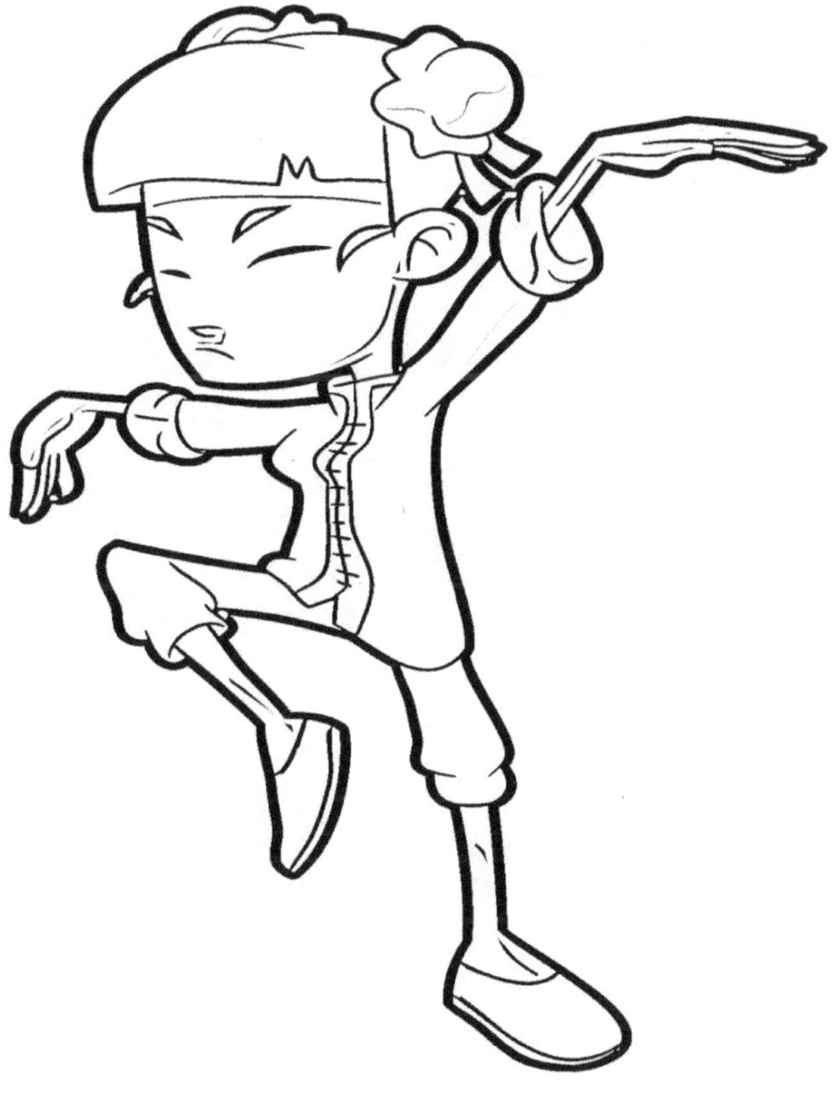

ButtWeasel

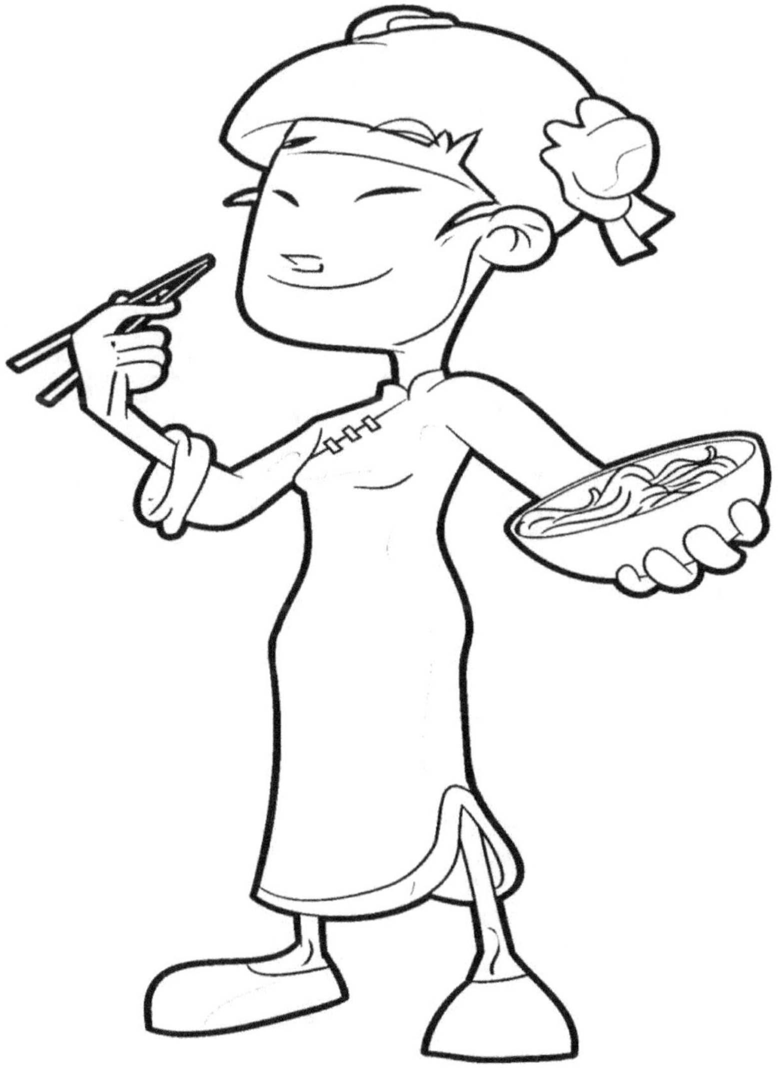

MuffMunch

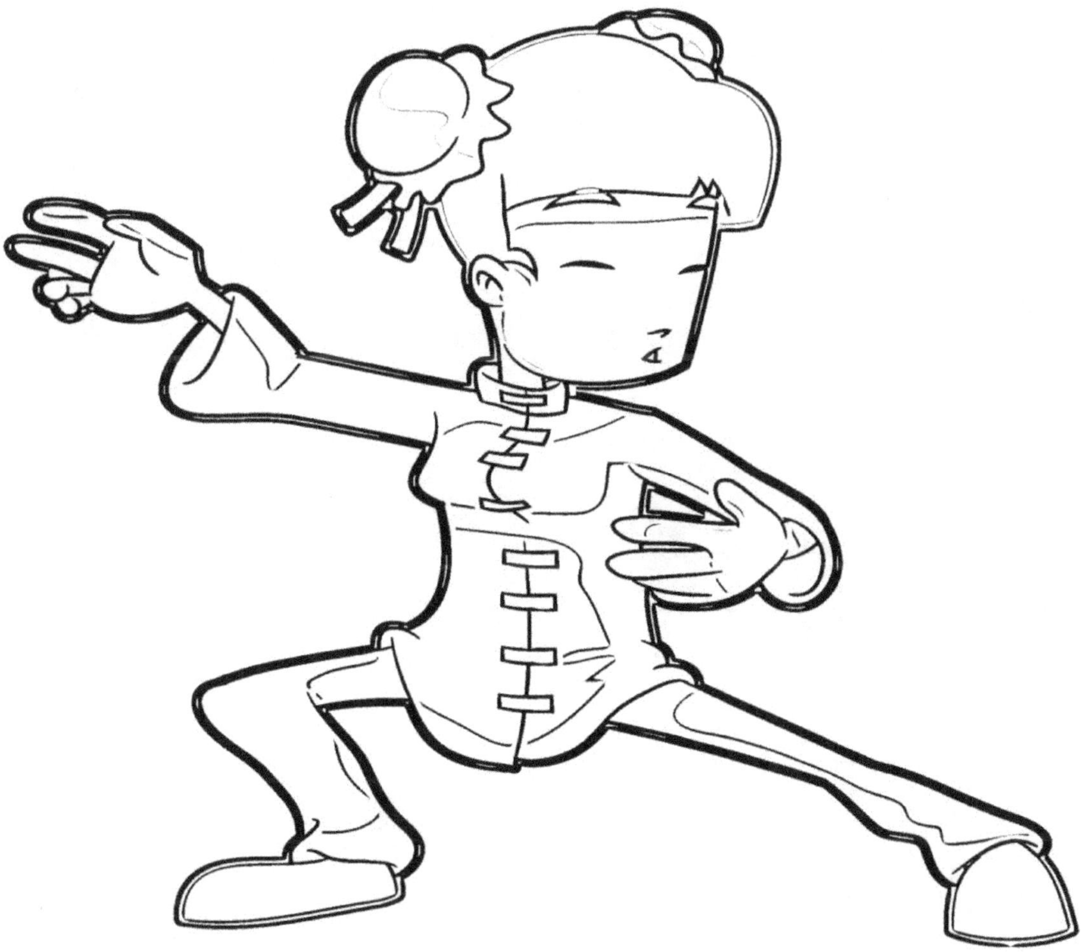

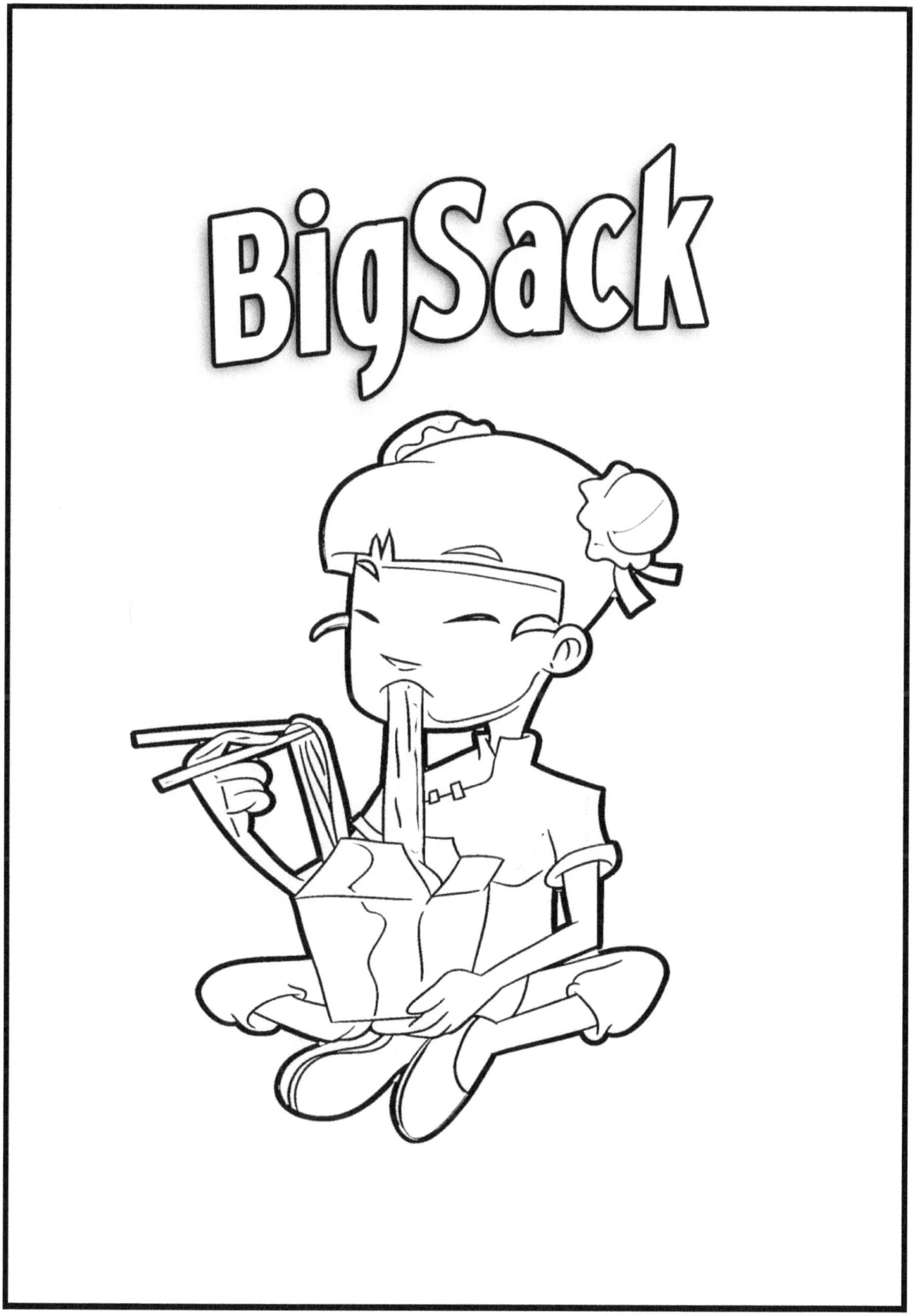
BigSack

ButtBurglar

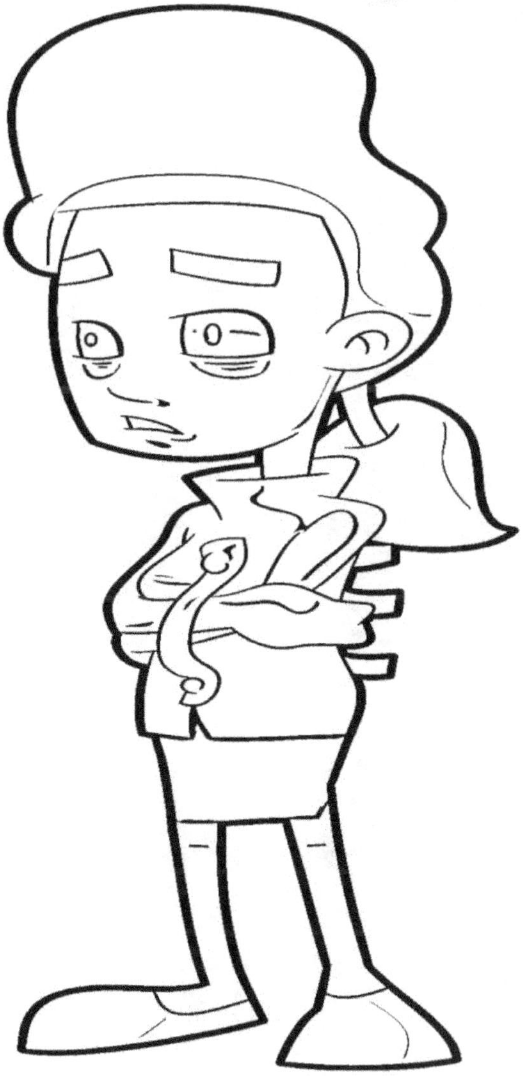

CrackFace

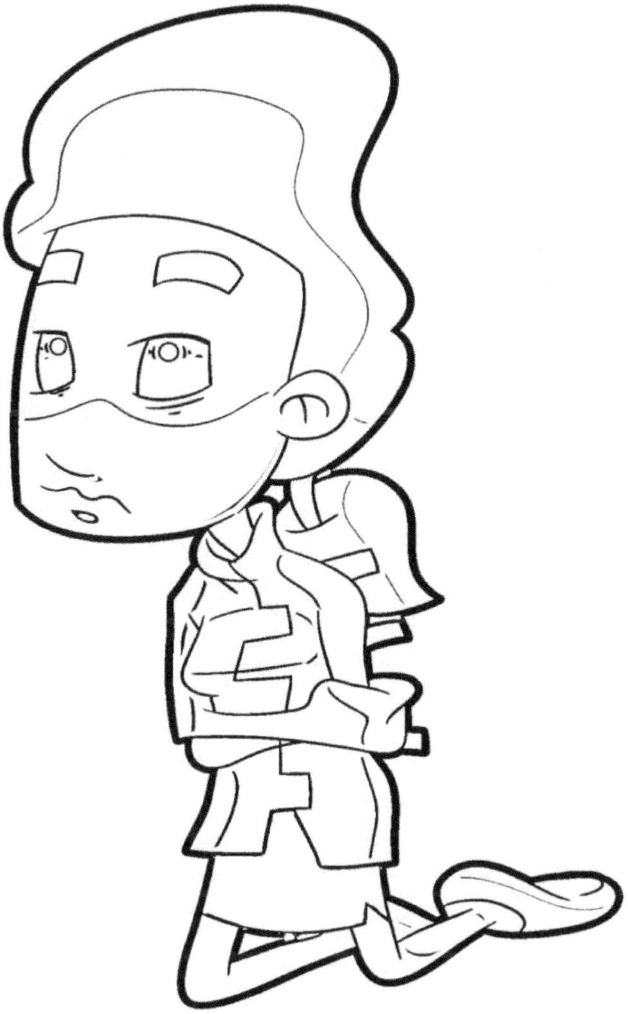

Sugar Tits

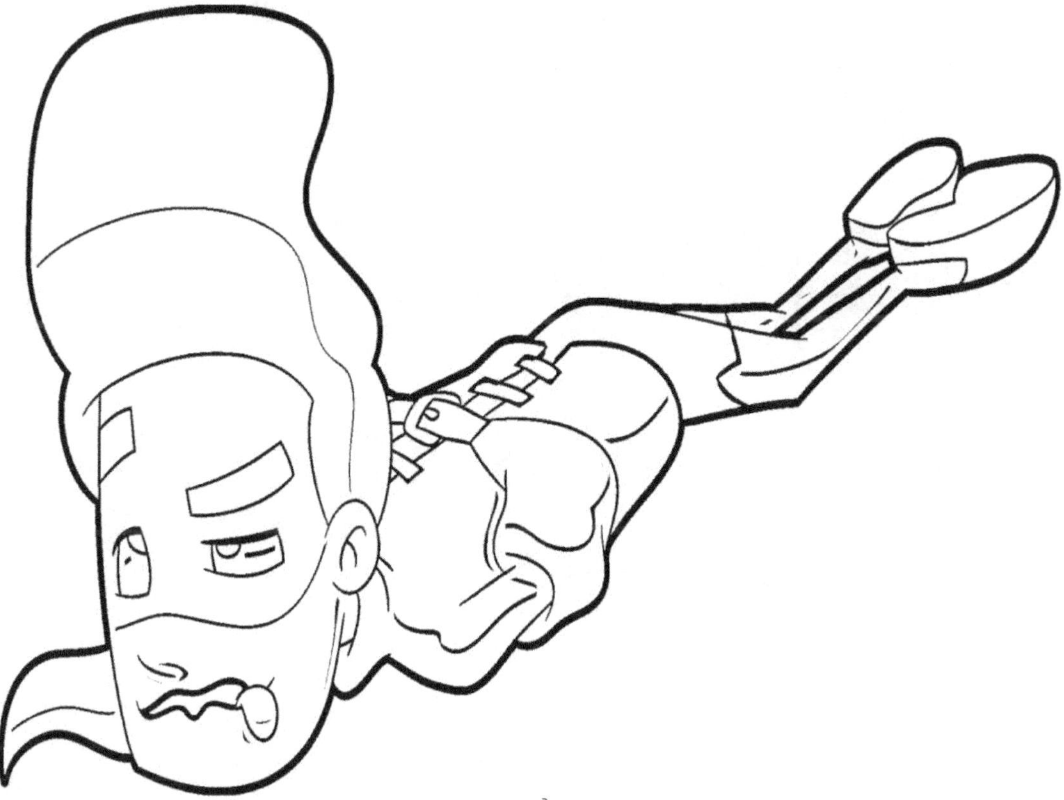

SackRider

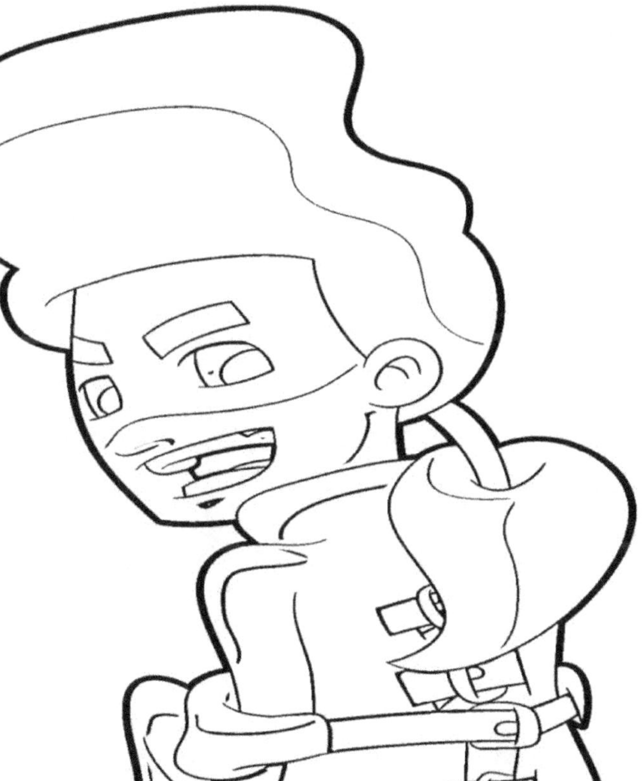

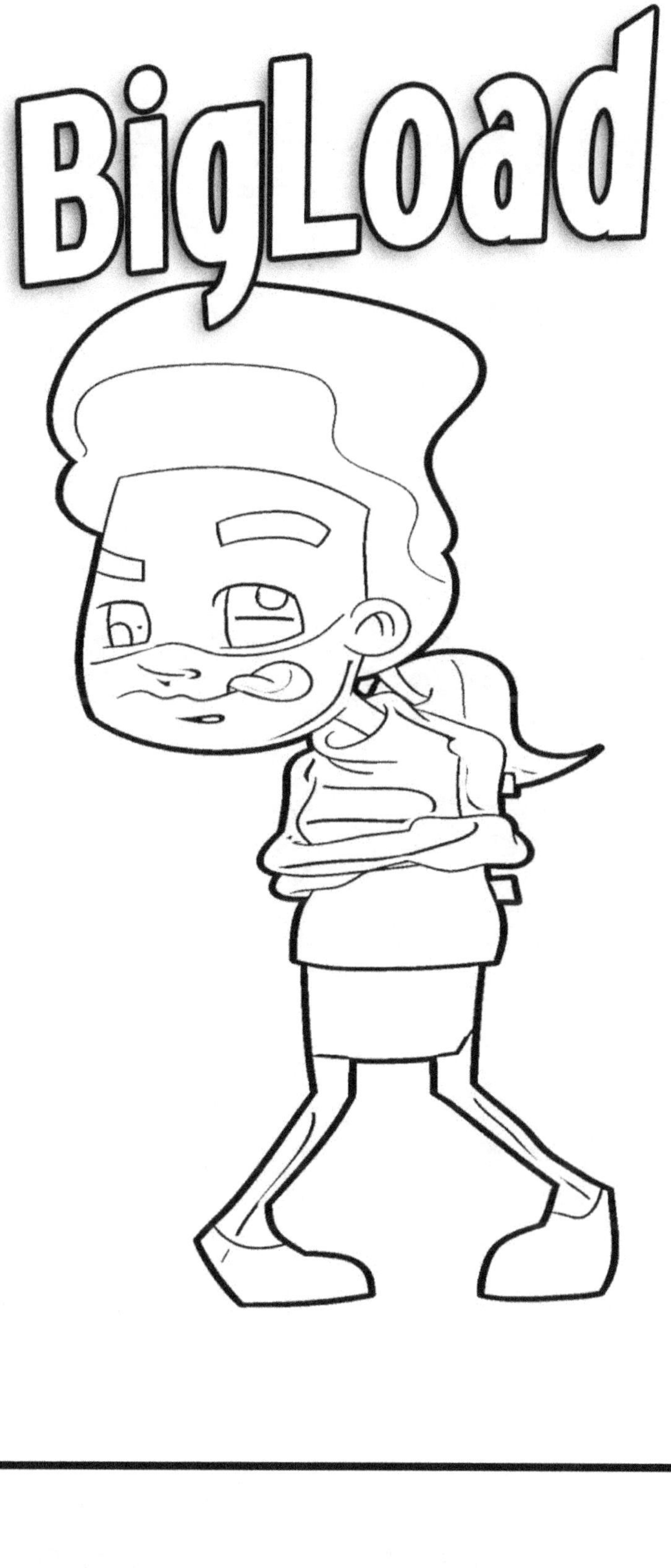
BigLoad

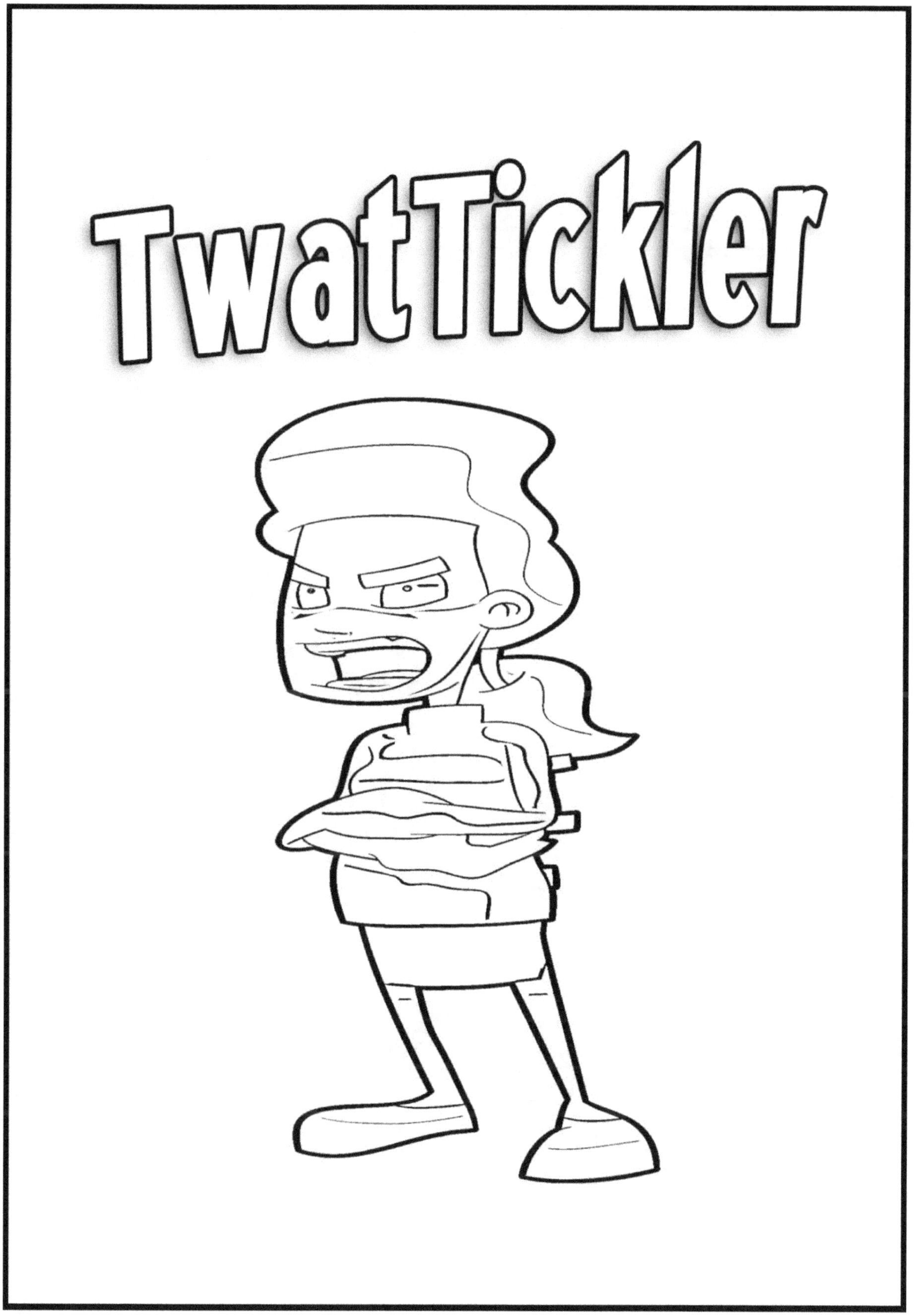
TwatTickler

SlickSnatch

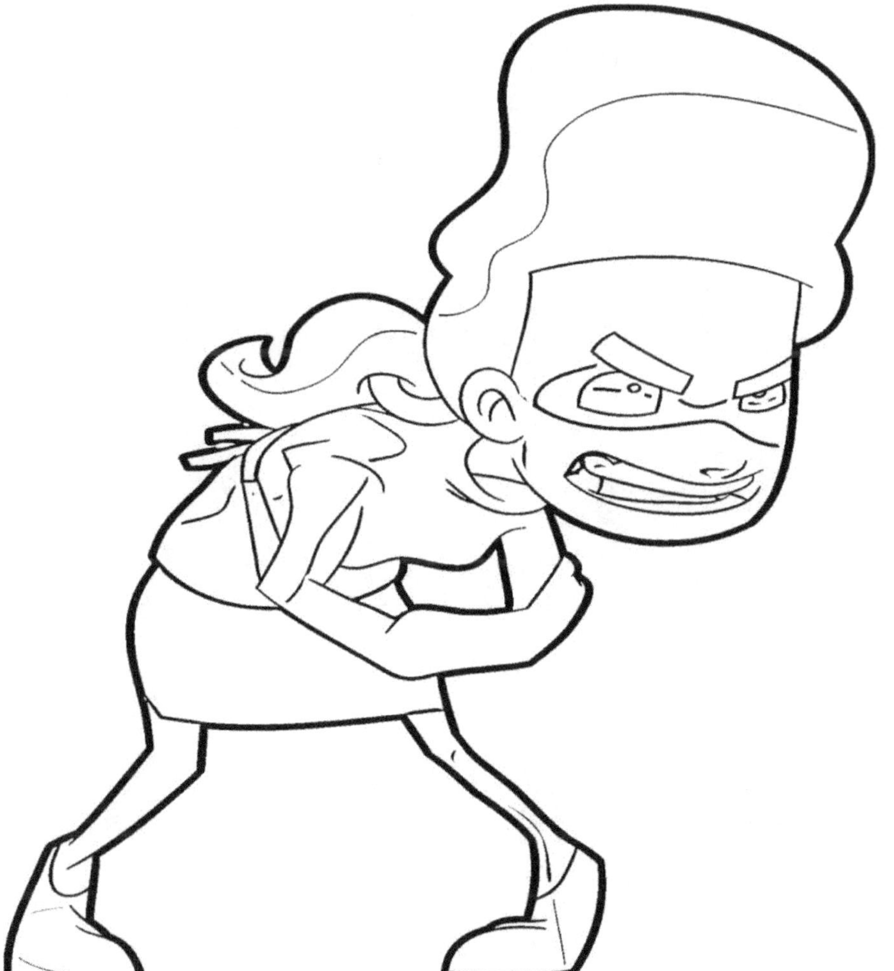

www.ingramcontent.com/pod-product-compliance
Lightning Source LLC
Chambersburg PA
CBHW080612190526
45169CB00007B/2980
* 9 7 8 1 5 3 0 9 2 2 6 1 1 *